GRAPHIC SCIENCE AND ENGINEERING IN ACTION

THE INCREDIBLE WORK OF ENGINEERS

WITH MAX AXIOM SUPER SCIENTIST

by Agnieszka Biskup

illustrated by Marcelo Baez

Consultant:
Morgan Hynes, PhD
Research Assistant Professor, Education
Research Program Manager
Center for Engineering Education and Outreach
Tufts University
Medford, Massachusetts

CAPSTONE PRESS
a capstone imprint

Graphic Library is published by Capstone Press,
1710 Roe Crest Drive, North Mankato, Minnesota 56003
www.capstonepub.com

Library of Congress Cataloging-in-Publication Data
Biskup, Agnieszka.
  The incredible work of engineers with Max Axiom, super scientist / by Agnieszka
Biskup ; illustrated by Marcelo Baez.
      p. cm.—(Graphic library. Graphic science and engineering in action)
  Includes bibliographical references and index.
  ISBN 978-1-4296-9937-2 (library binding)
  ISBN 978-1-62065-705-8 (paperback)
  ISBN 978-1-4765-1591-5 (ebook PDF)
  1. Engineering—Comic books, strips, etc.—Juvenile literature. 2. Graphic novels. I.
Baez, Marcelo, illustrator. II. Title.
  TA149.B57 2013
  620.0023—dc23   2012026439

Summary: In graphic novel format, follows the adventures of Max Axiom as he learns
about what engineers do and how they work.

Designer
Ted Williams

Media Researcher
Wanda Winch

Production Specialist
Laura Manthe

Editor
Christopher L. Harbo

Printed in the United States of America in Brainerd, Minnesota.
092012   006938BANGS13

Table of Contents

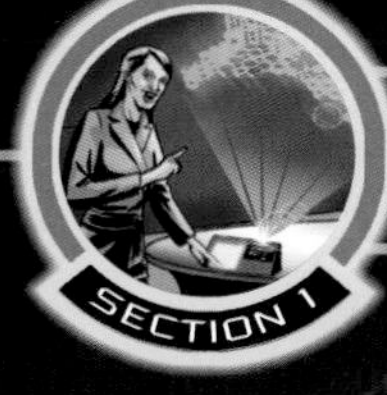
SECTION 1

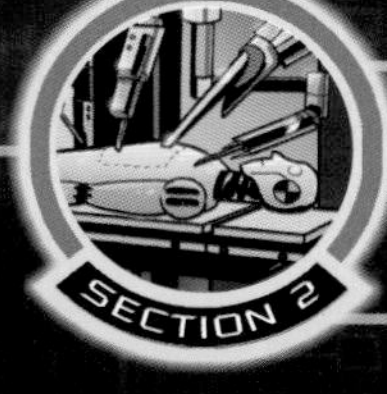
SECTION 2

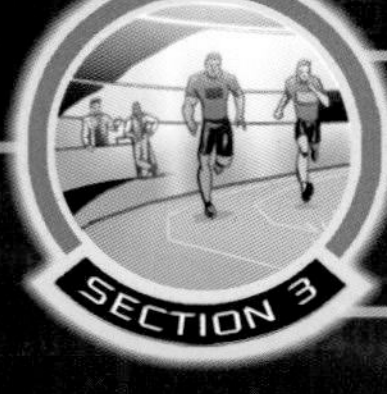
SECTION 3

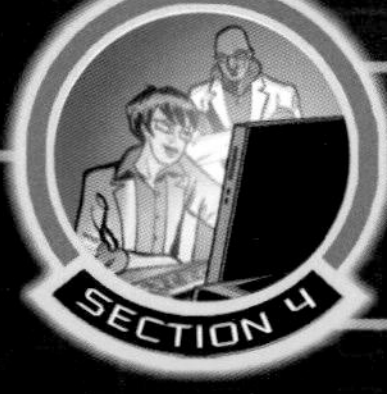
SECTION 4

A MISSION FOR MAX

Super Scientist Max Axiom races to the Federal Space Exploration Agency for an appointment with its director.

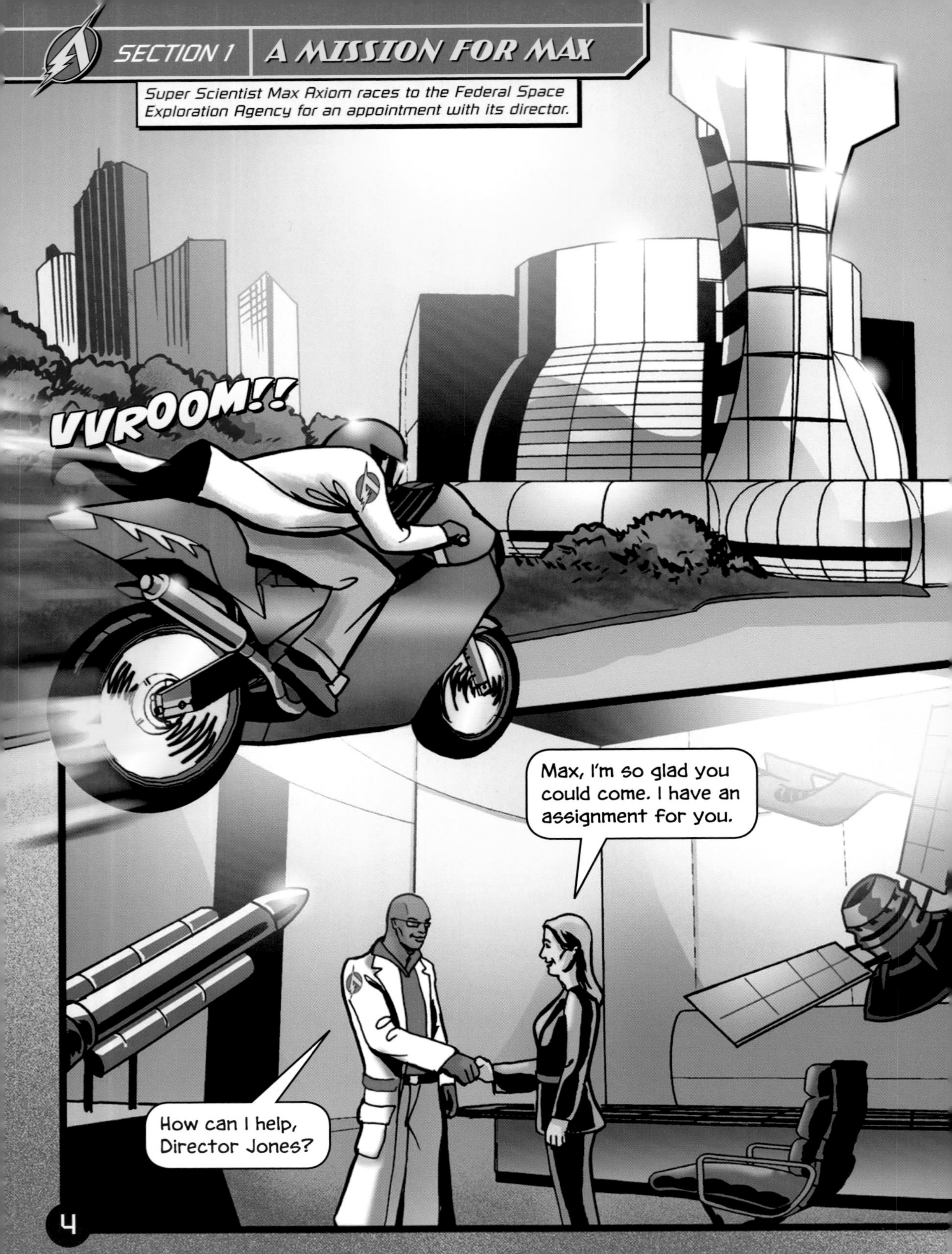
VVROOM!!
Max, I'm so glad you could come. I have an assignment for you.
How can I help, Director Jones?

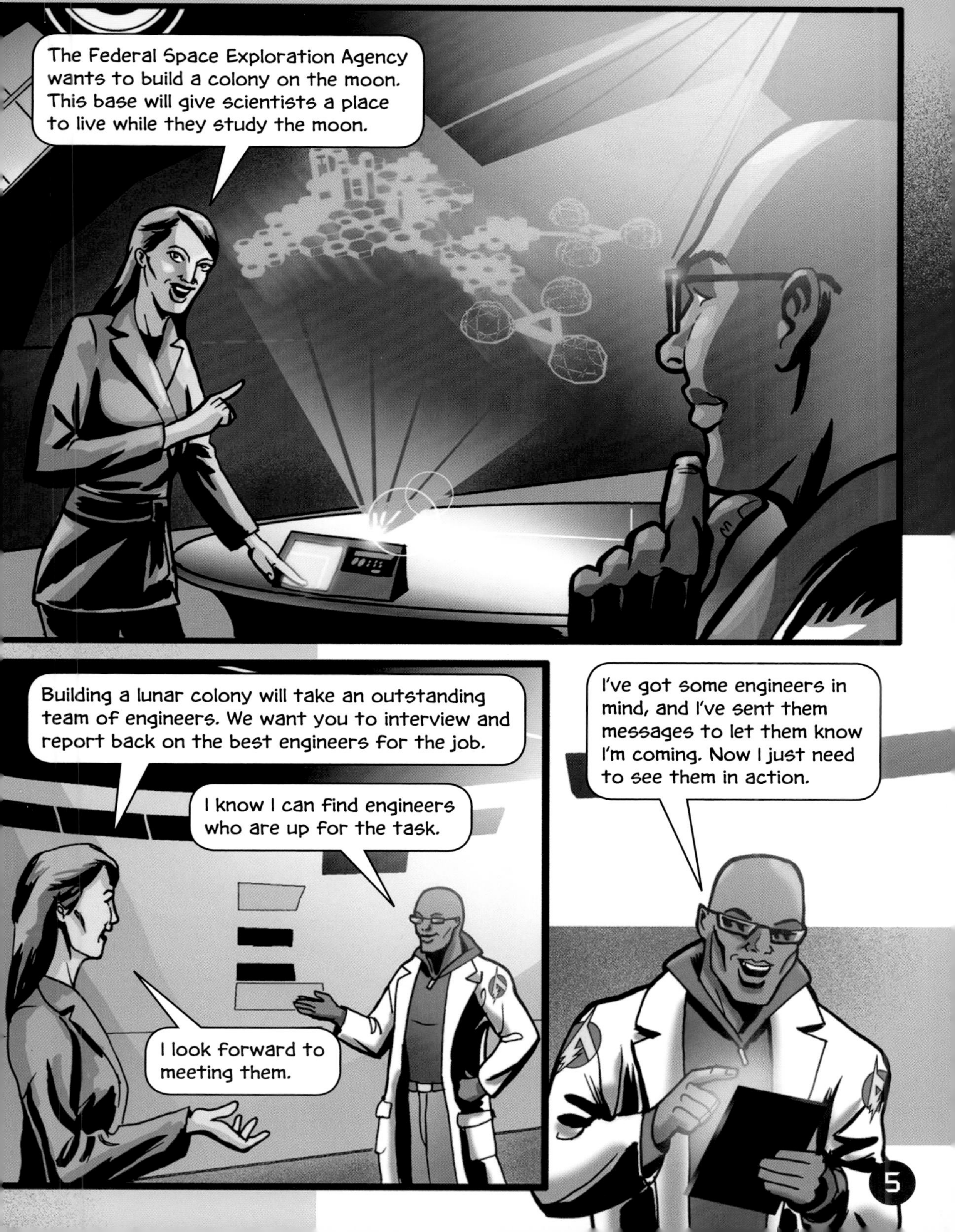
The Federal Space Exploration Agency wants to build a colony on the moon. This base will give scientists a place to live while they study the moon.
Building a lunar colony will take an outstanding team of engineers. We want you to interview and report back on the best engineers for the job.
I know I can find engineers who are up for the task.
I look forward to meeting them.
I've got some engineers in mind, and I've sent them messages to let them know I'm coming. Now I just need to see them in action.

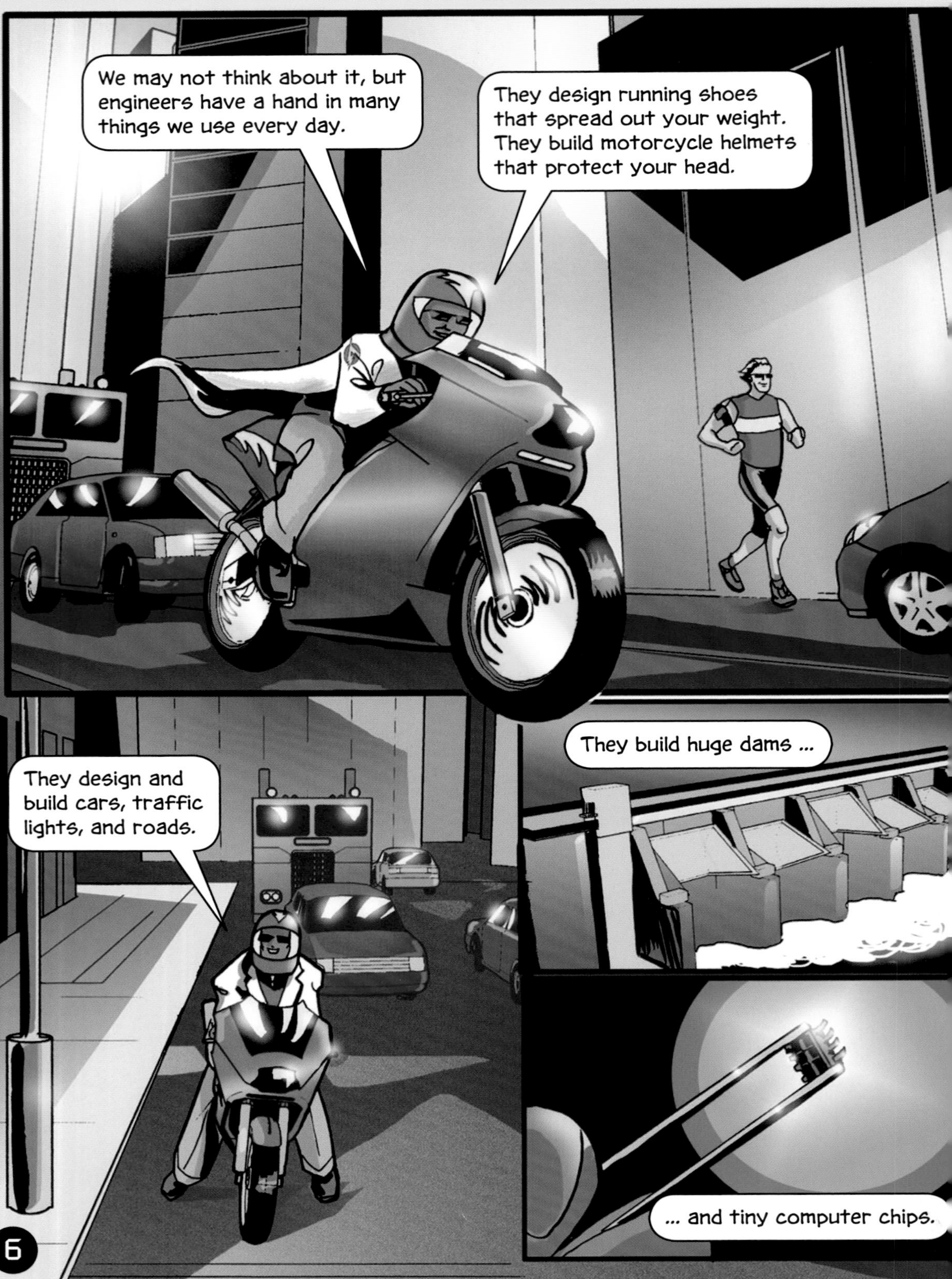
We may not think about it, but engineers have a hand in many things we use every day.
They design running shoes that spread out your weight. They build motorcycle helmets that protect your head.
They design and build cars, traffic lights, and roads.
They build huge dams ...
... and tiny computer chips.

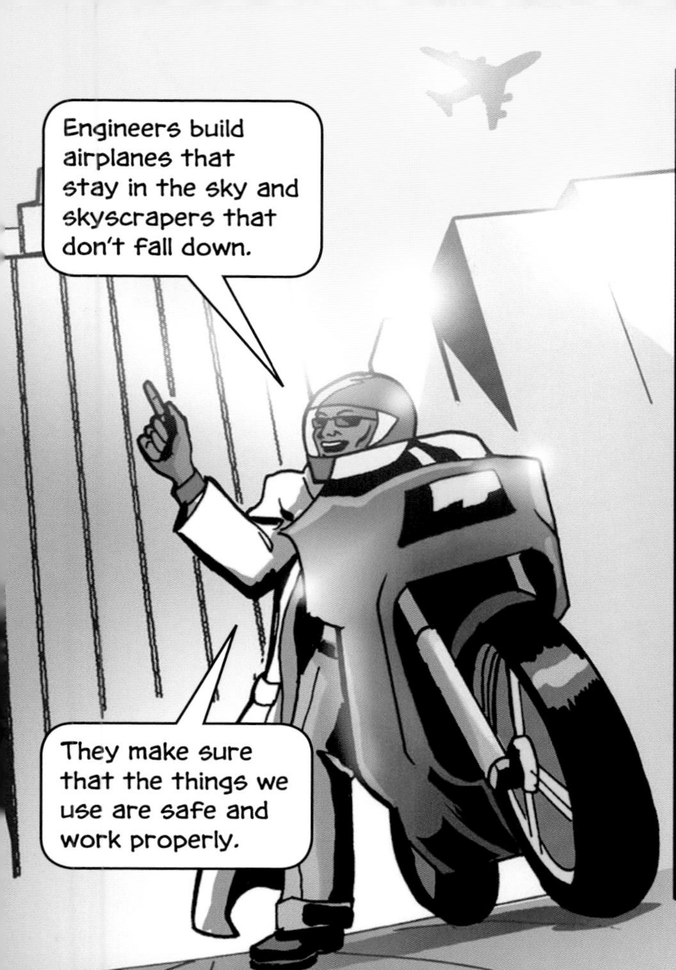
Engineers build airplanes that stay in the sky and skyscrapers that don't fall down.
They make sure that the things we use are safe and work properly.

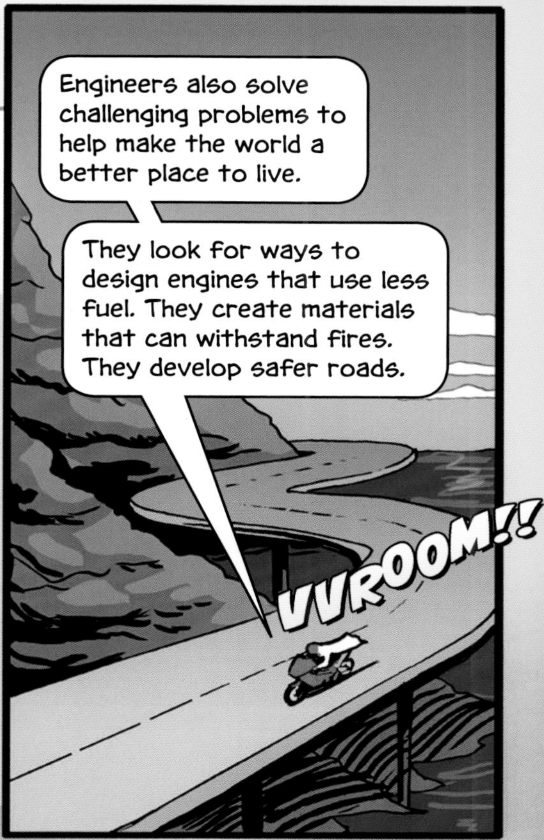
Engineers also solve challenging problems to help make the world a better place to live.
They look for ways to design engines that use less fuel. They create materials that can withstand fires. They develop safer roads.
VVROOM!!

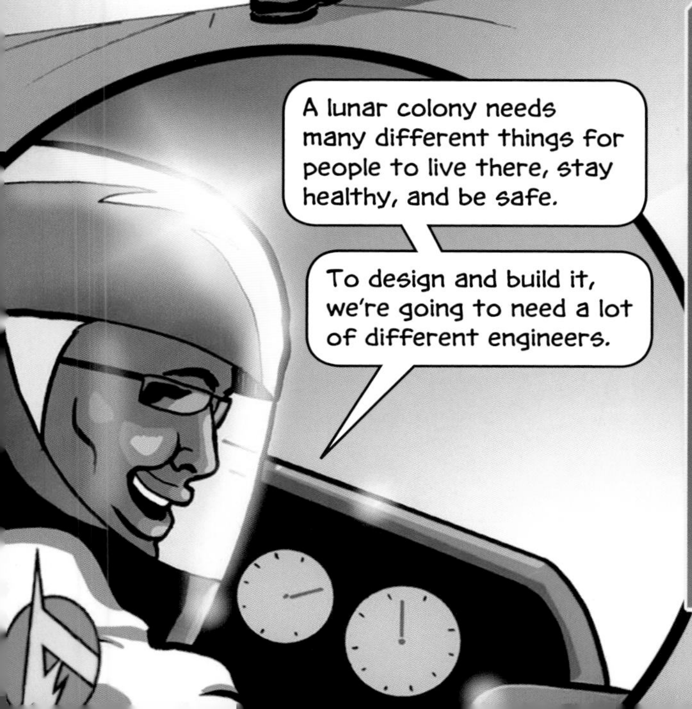
A lunar colony needs many different things for people to live there, stay healthy, and be safe.
To design and build it, we're going to need a lot of different engineers.

Scientist vs. Engineer

Scientists and engineers are not the same thing. An engineer once said scientists discover the world that exists and engineers create the world that never was. But scientists and engineers often work together. Engineers use science to build things that haven't existed before. And scientists need engineers to design and build the instruments and tools they use to make their discoveries.

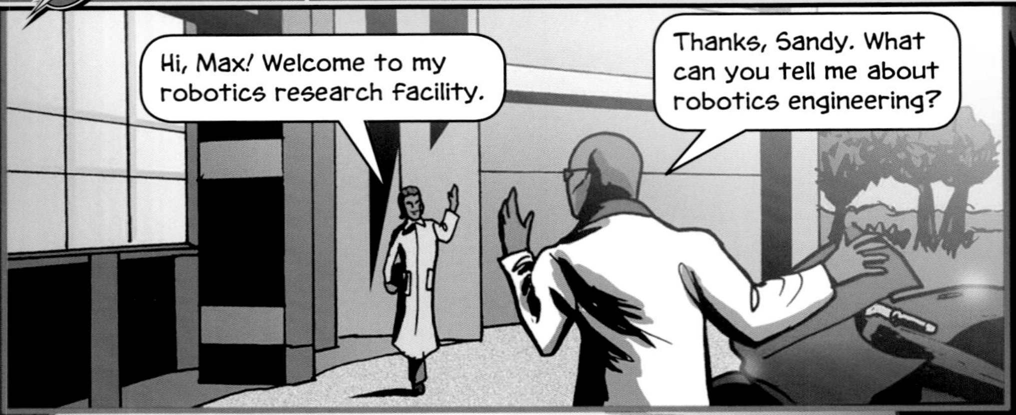
Hi, Max! Welcome to my robotics research facility.
Thanks, Sandy. What can you tell me about robotics engineering?

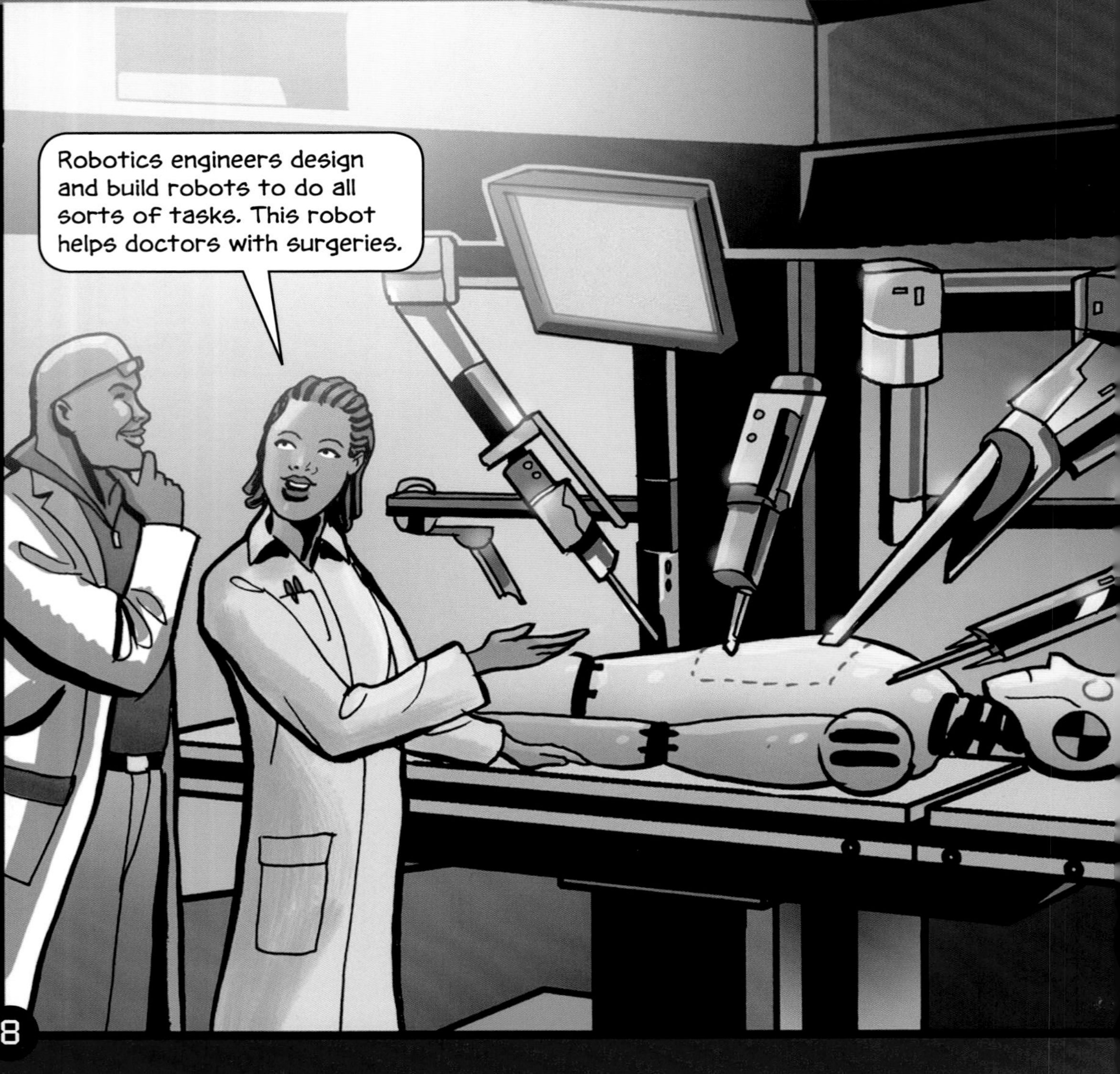
Robotics engineers design and build robots to do all sorts of tasks. This robot helps doctors with surgeries.

Some robots do jobs that are too dangerous for people. This remote-controlled robot disarms bombs.

Other robots explore the ocean, volcanoes, or even other planets.

Could robots help build a lunar colony?

You bet! Robots don't need spacesuits or air to breathe. With the right tools, they could help prepare the building site on the moon.

ROBOTS ON THE MOVE

Engineers design and build robots that move in many ways. There are robots that swim, hop, climb, and walk. While some walking robots have two legs, engineers also use ideas from the insect world. Six-legged robots are very stable. Sometimes six legs work better than two!

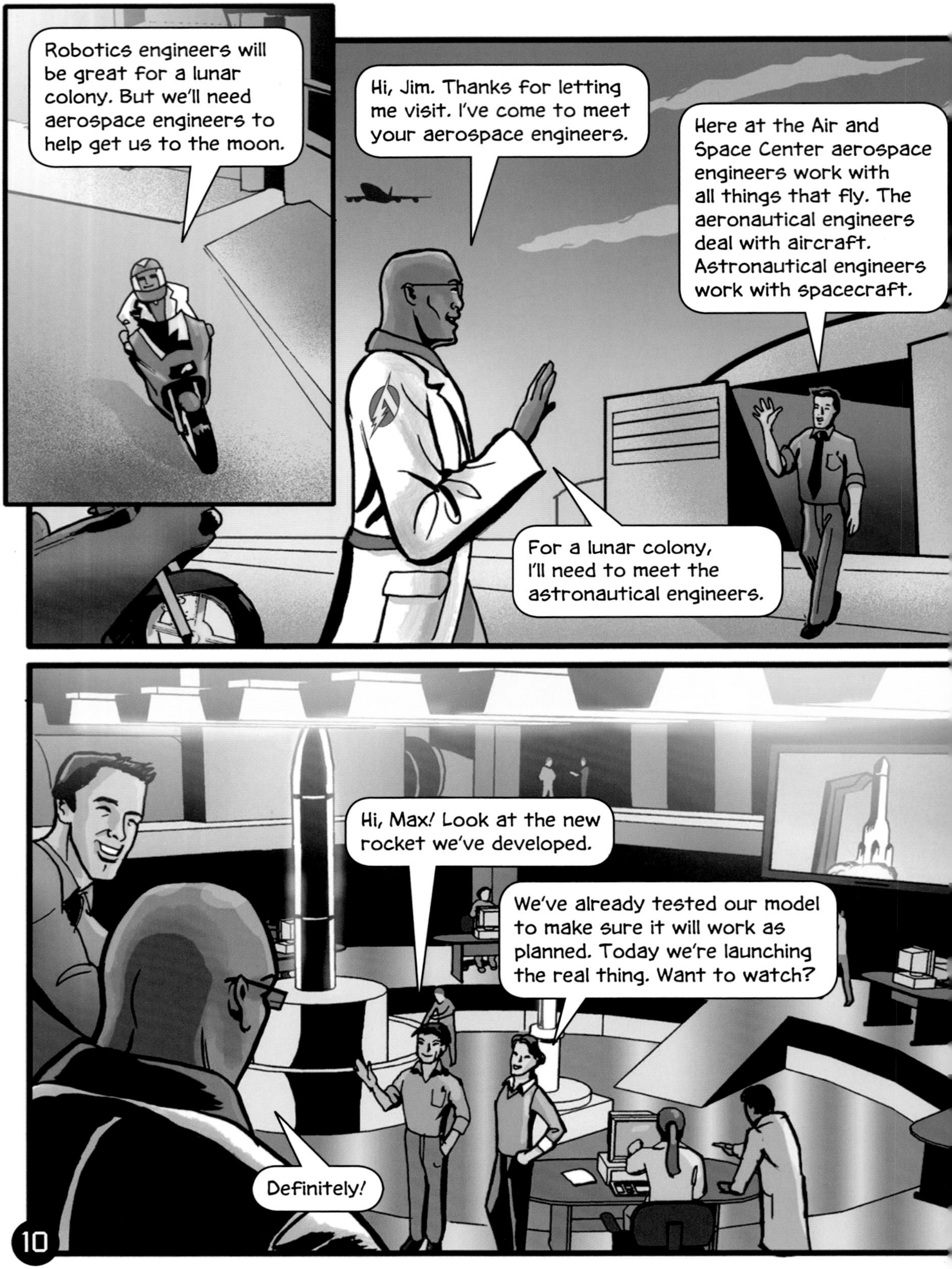
Robotics engineers will be great for a lunar colony. But we'll need aerospace engineers to help get us to the moon.
Hi, Jim. Thanks for letting me visit. I've come to meet your aerospace engineers.
Here at the Air and Space Center aerospace engineers work with all things that fly. The aeronautical engineers deal with aircraft. Astronautical engineers work with spacecraft.
For a lunar colony, I'll need to meet the astronautical engineers.
Hi, Max! Look at the new rocket we've developed.
We've already tested our model to make sure it will work as planned. Today we're launching the real thing. Want to watch?
Definitely!

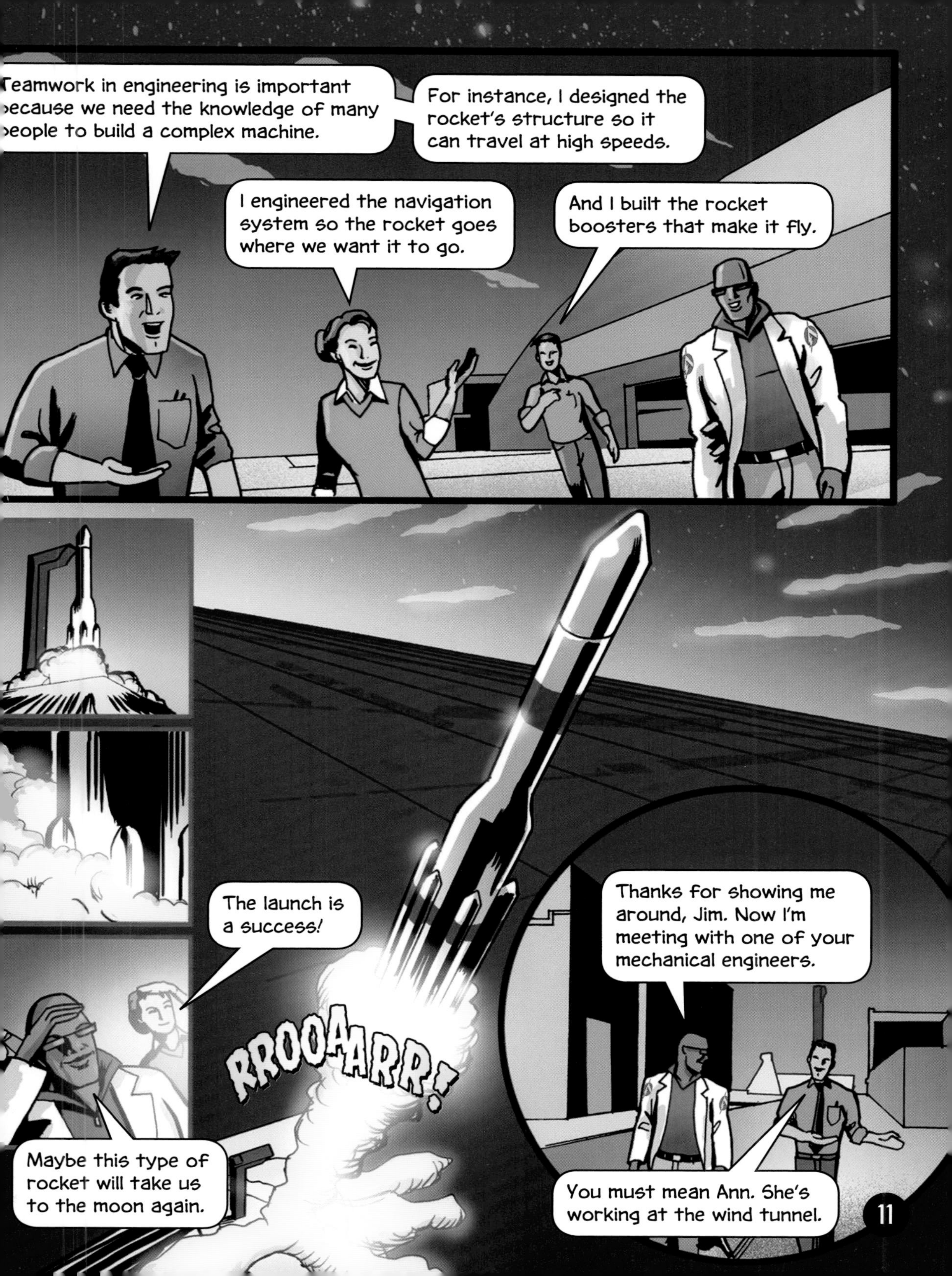

Teamwork in engineering is important because we need the knowledge of many people to build a complex machine.
For instance, I designed the rocket's structure so it can travel at high speeds.
I engineered the navigation system so the rocket goes where we want it to go.
And I built the rocket boosters that make it fly.
RROOAARR!
The launch is a success!
Maybe this type of rocket will take us to the moon again.
Thanks for showing me around, Jim. Now I'm meeting with one of your mechanical engineers.
You must mean Ann. She's working at the wind tunnel.

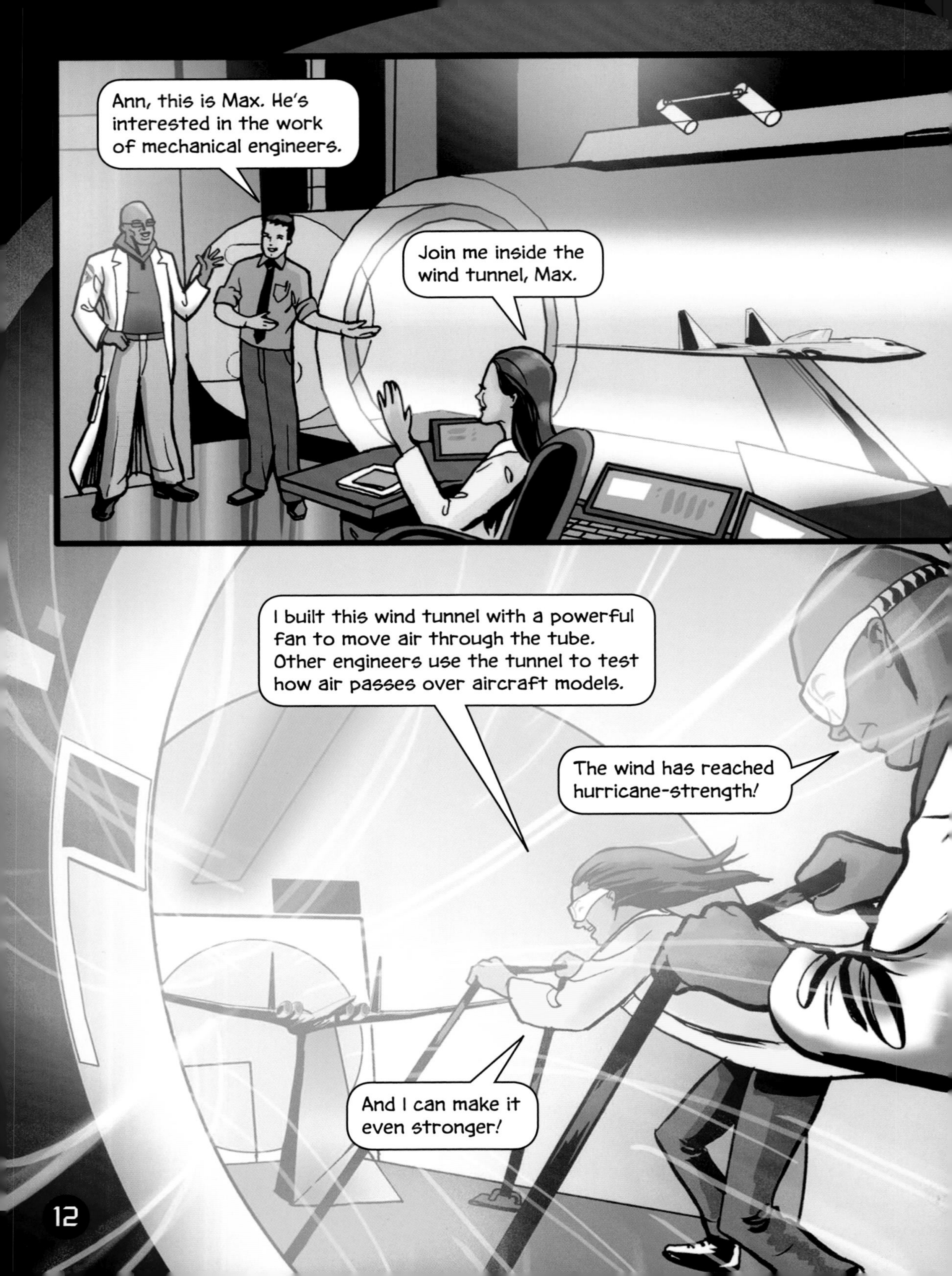
Ann, this is Max. He's interested in the work of mechanical engineers.
Join me inside the wind tunnel, Max.
I built this wind tunnel with a powerful fan to move air through the tube. Other engineers use the tunnel to test how air passes over aircraft models.
The wind has reached hurricane-strength!
And I can make it even stronger!

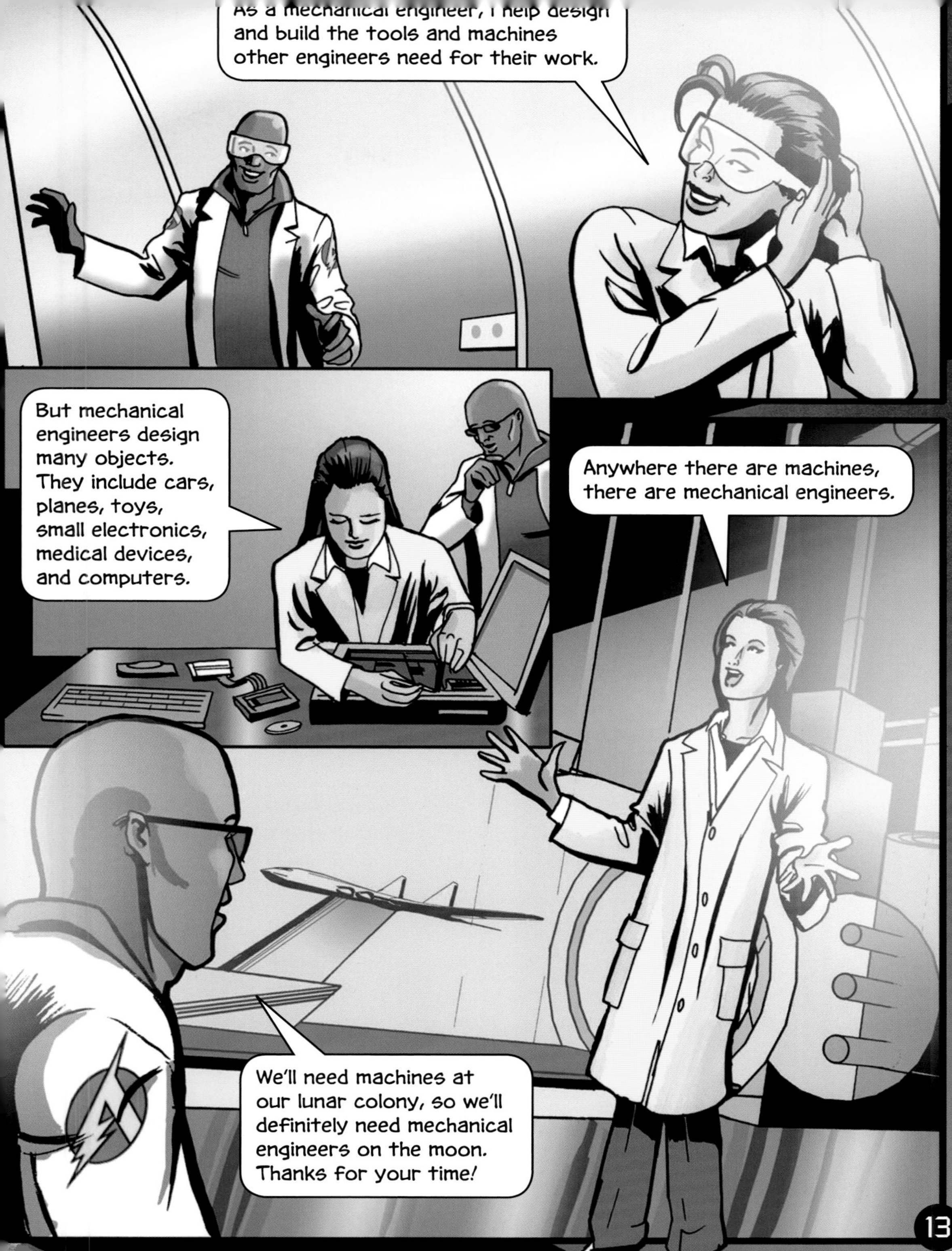
As a mechanical engineer, I help design and build the tools and machines other engineers need for their work.
But mechanical engineers design many objects. They include cars, planes, toys, small electronics, medical devices, and computers.
Anywhere there are machines, there are mechanical engineers.
We'll need machines at our lunar colony, so we'll definitely need mechanical engineers on the moon. Thanks for your time!

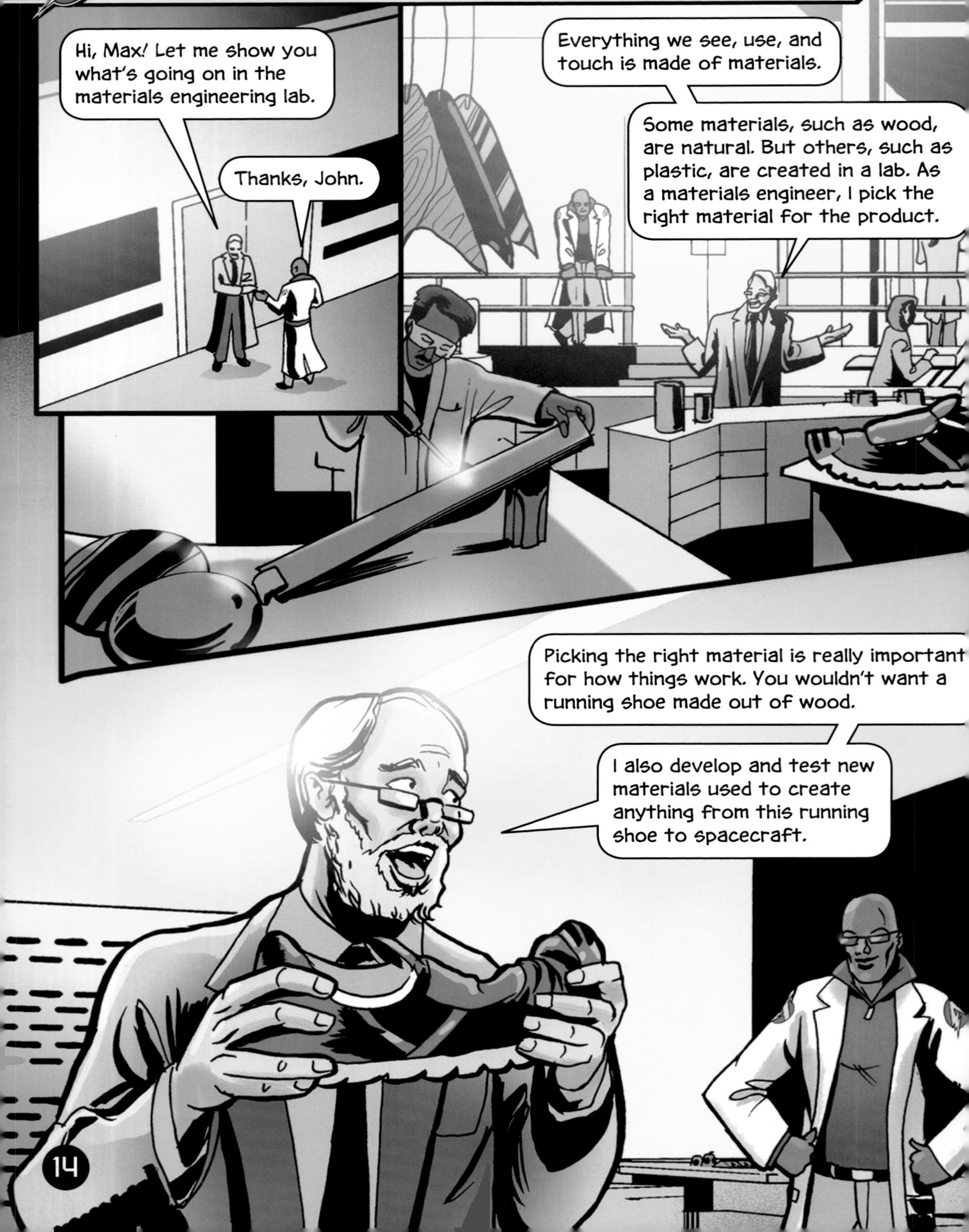
Hi, Max! Let me show you what's going on in the materials engineering lab.
Thanks, John.
Everything we see, use, and touch is made of materials.
Some materials, such as wood, are natural. But others, such as plastic, are created in a lab. As a materials engineer, I pick the right material for the product.
Picking the right material is really important for how things work. You wouldn't want a running shoe made out of wood.
I also develop and test new materials used to create anything from this running shoe to spacecraft.

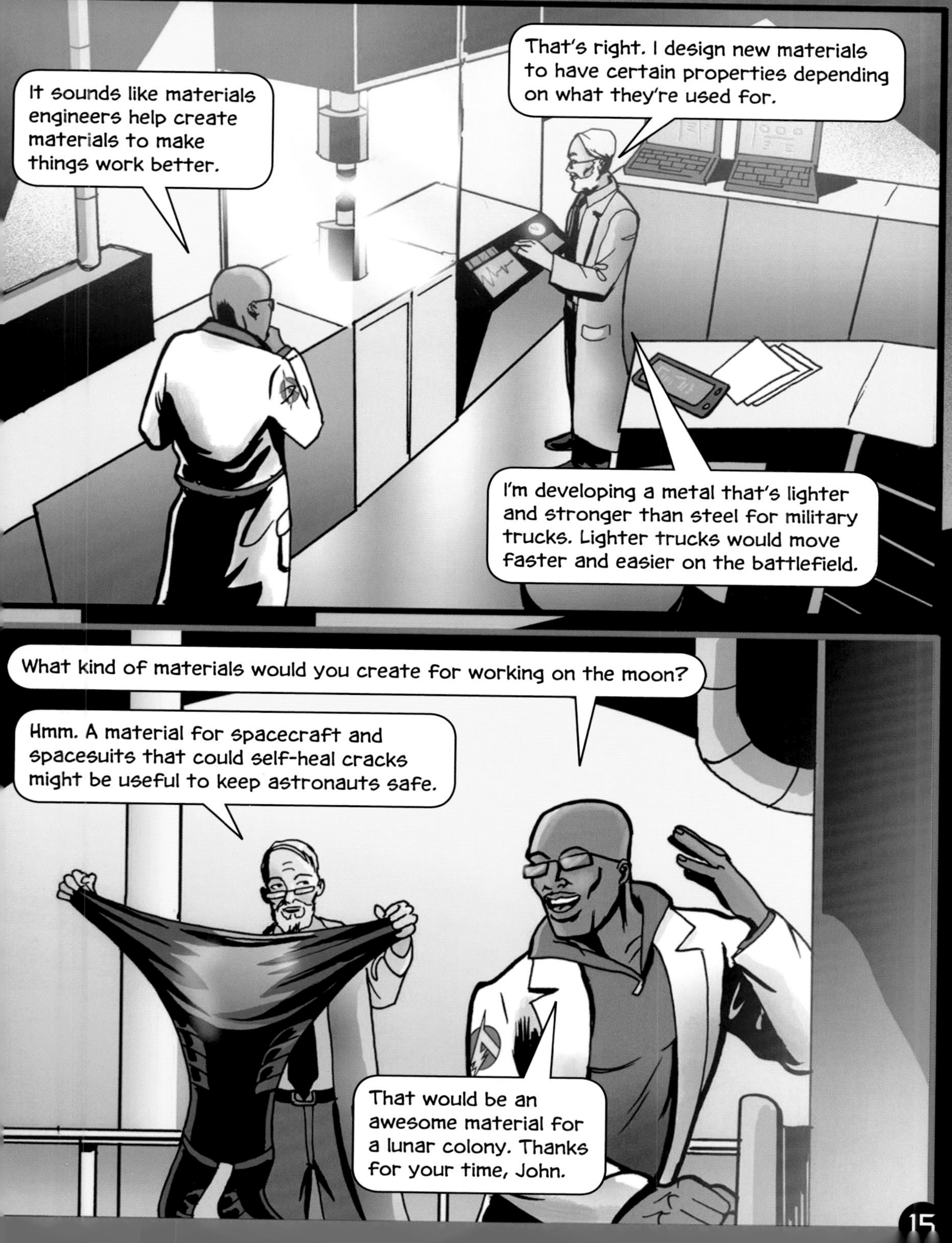
It sounds like materials engineers help create materials to make things work better.
That's right. I design new materials to have certain properties depending on what they're used for.
I'm developing a metal that's lighter and stronger than steel for military trucks. Lighter trucks would move faster and easier on the battlefield.
What kind of materials would you create for working on the moon?
Hmm. A material for spacecraft and spacesuits that could self-heal cracks might be useful to keep astronauts safe.
That would be an awesome material for a lunar colony. Thanks for your time, John.

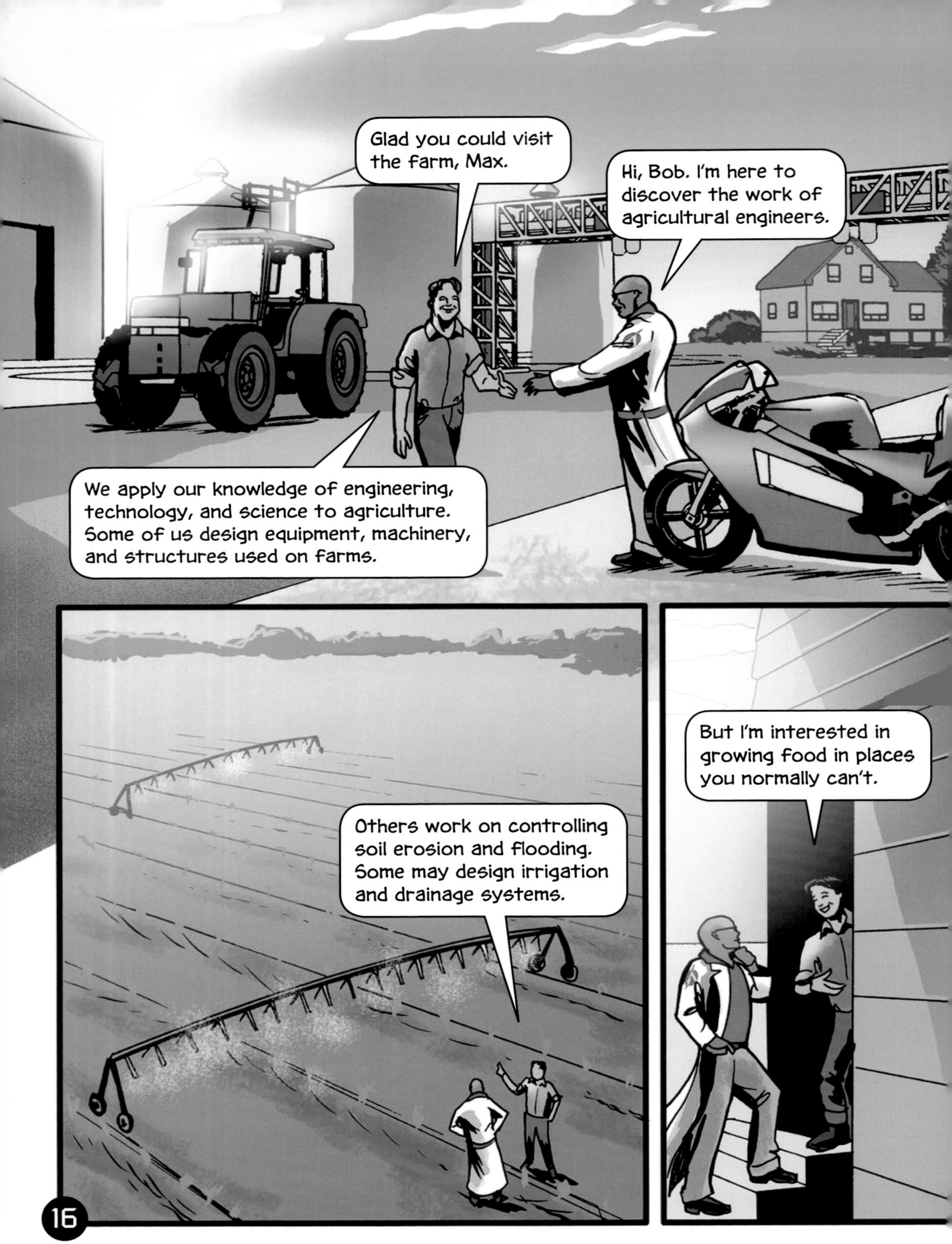
Glad you could visit the farm, Max.
Hi, Bob. I'm here to discover the work of agricultural engineers.
We apply our knowledge of engineering, technology, and science to agriculture. Some of us design equipment, machinery, and structures used on farms.
Others work on controlling soil erosion and flooding. Some may design irrigation and drainage systems.
But I'm interested in growing food in places you normally can't.

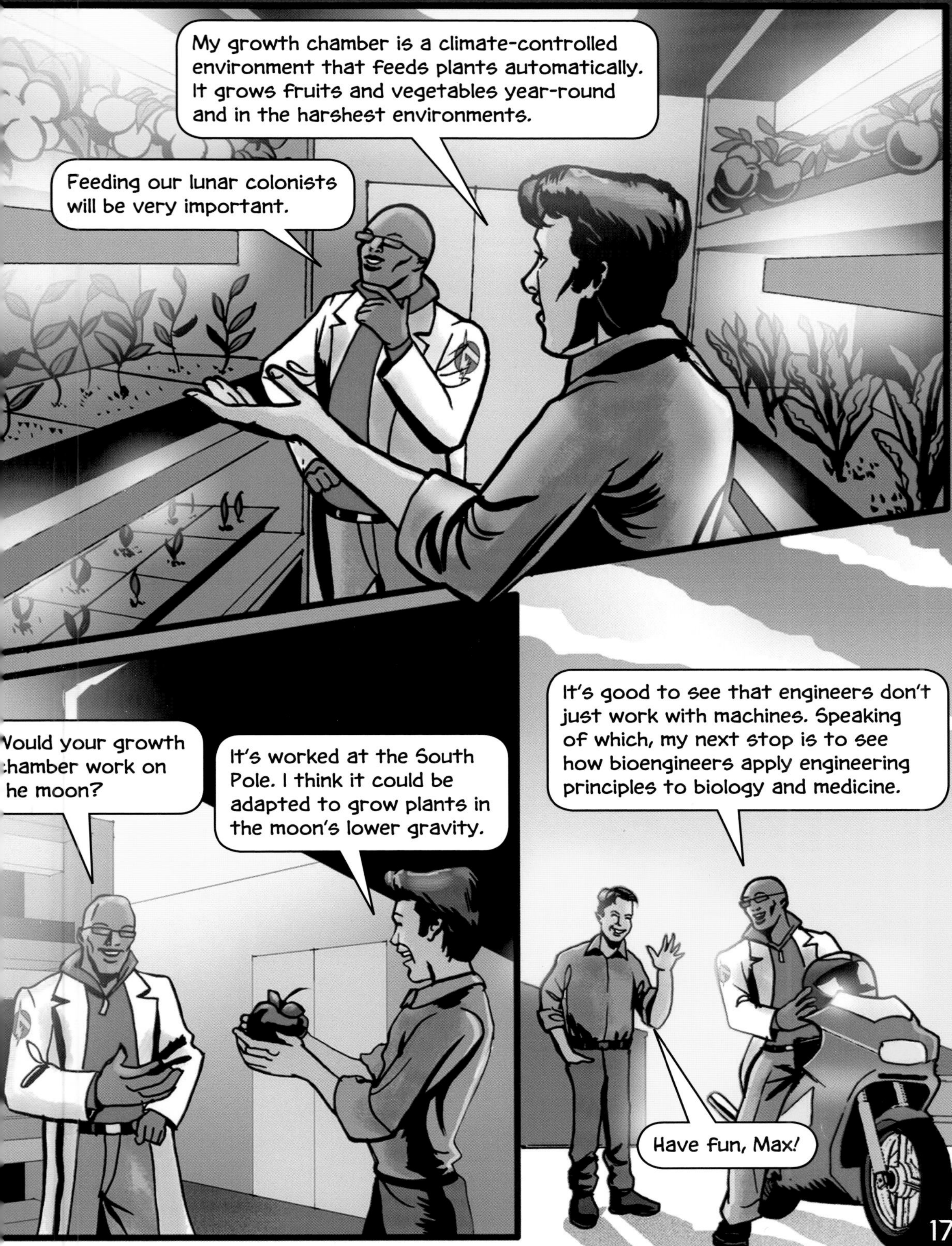
My growth chamber is a climate-controlled environment that feeds plants automatically. It grows fruits and vegetables year-round and in the harshest environments.
Feeding our lunar colonists will be very important.
Would your growth chamber work on the moon?
It's worked at the South Pole. I think it could be adapted to grow plants in the moon's lower gravity.
It's good to see that engineers don't just work with machines. Speaking of which, my next stop is to see how bioengineers apply engineering principles to biology and medicine.
Have fun, Max!

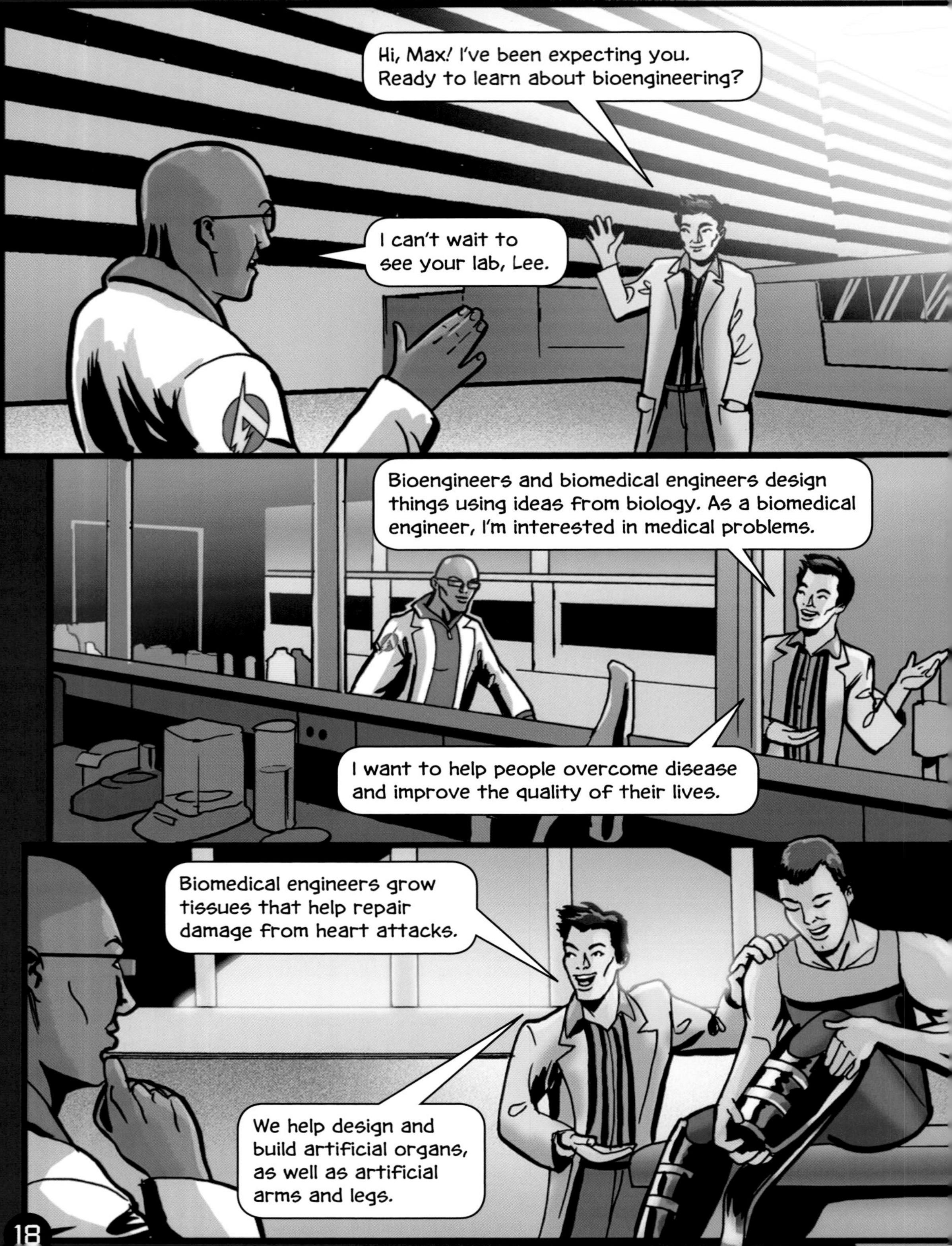
Hi, Max! I've been expecting you. Ready to learn about bioengineering?
I can't wait to see your lab, Lee.
Bioengineers and biomedical engineers design things using ideas from biology. As a biomedical engineer, I'm interested in medical problems.
I want to help people overcome disease and improve the quality of their lives.
Biomedical engineers grow tissues that help repair damage from heart attacks.
We help design and build artificial organs, as well as artificial arms and legs.

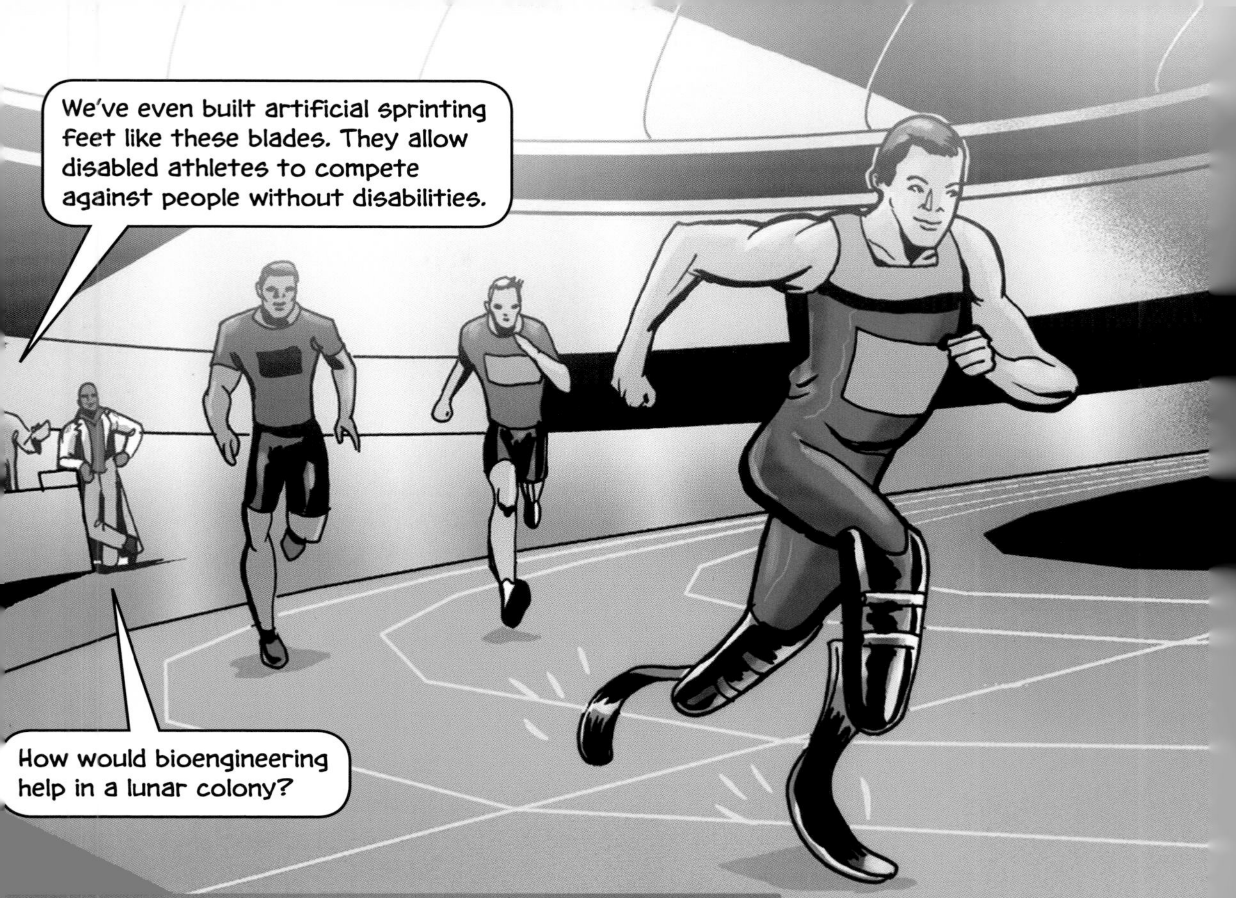
We've even built artificial sprinting feet like these blades. They allow disabled athletes to compete against people without disabilities.
How would bioengineering help in a lunar colony?

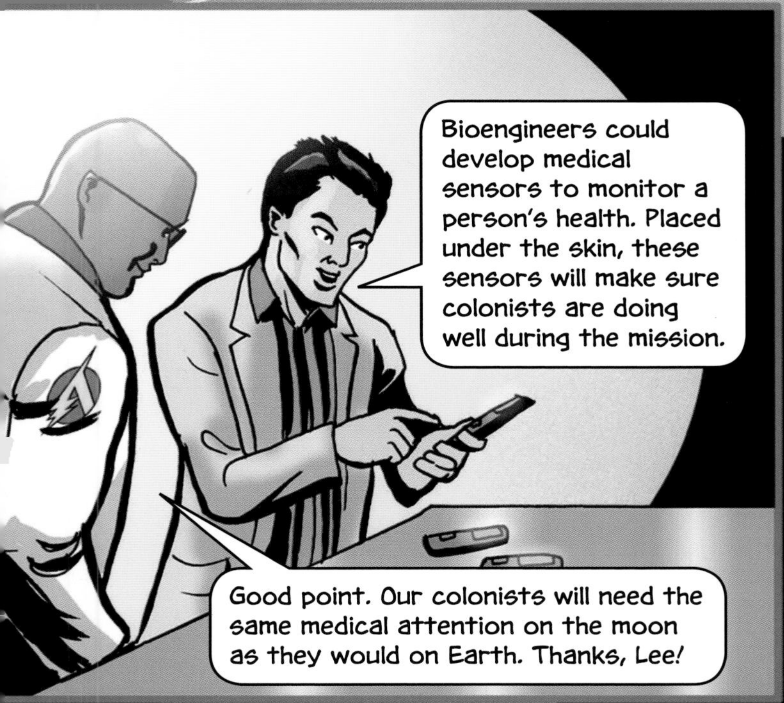
Bioengineers could develop medical sensors to monitor a person's health. Placed under the skin, these sensors will make sure colonists are doing well during the mission.
Good point. Our colonists will need the same medical attention on the moon as they would on Earth. Thanks, Lee!

Seeing Inside the Body

Bioengineers also design scanning systems for the human body. A CT scanner is a special X-ray machine. It takes hundreds of pictures to create a 3D image of a person's body. Doctors use CT scans to help diagnose disease.

CHEMICALS, SKYSCRAPERS, AND COMPUTERS

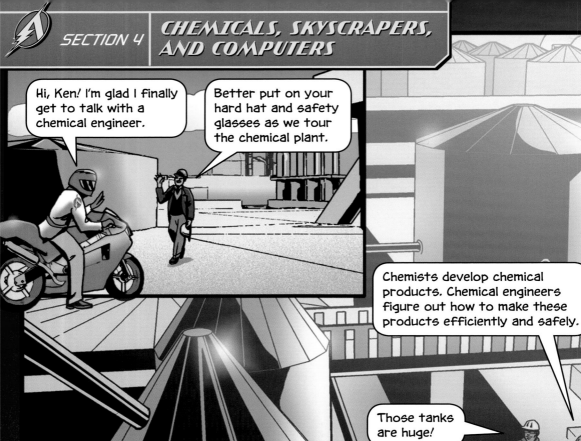

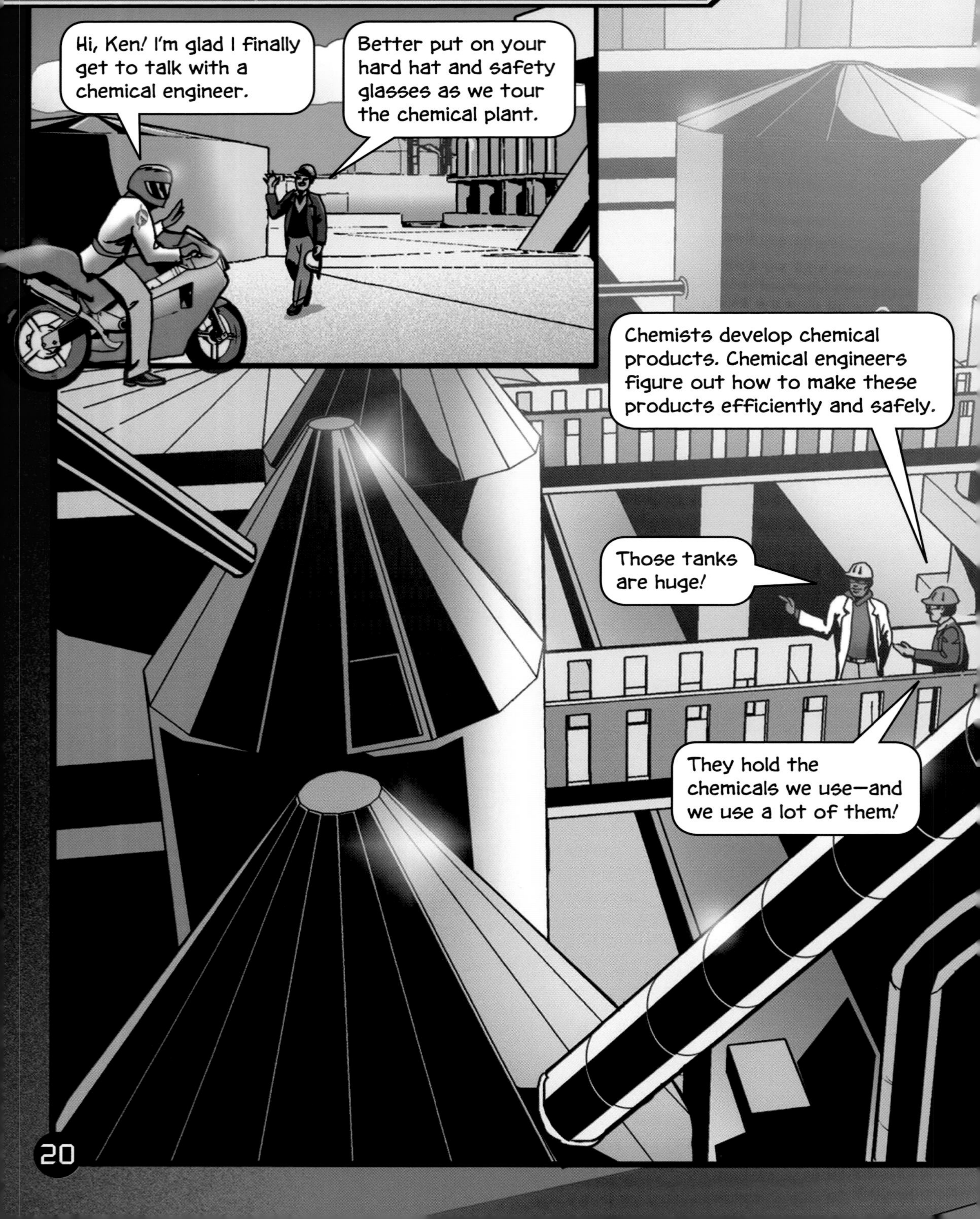

Hi, Ken! I'm glad I finally get to talk with a chemical engineer.

Better put on your hard hat and safety glasses as we tour the chemical plant.

Chemists develop chemical products. Chemical engineers figure out how to make these products efficiently and safely.

Those tanks are huge!

They hold the chemicals we use—and we use a lot of them!

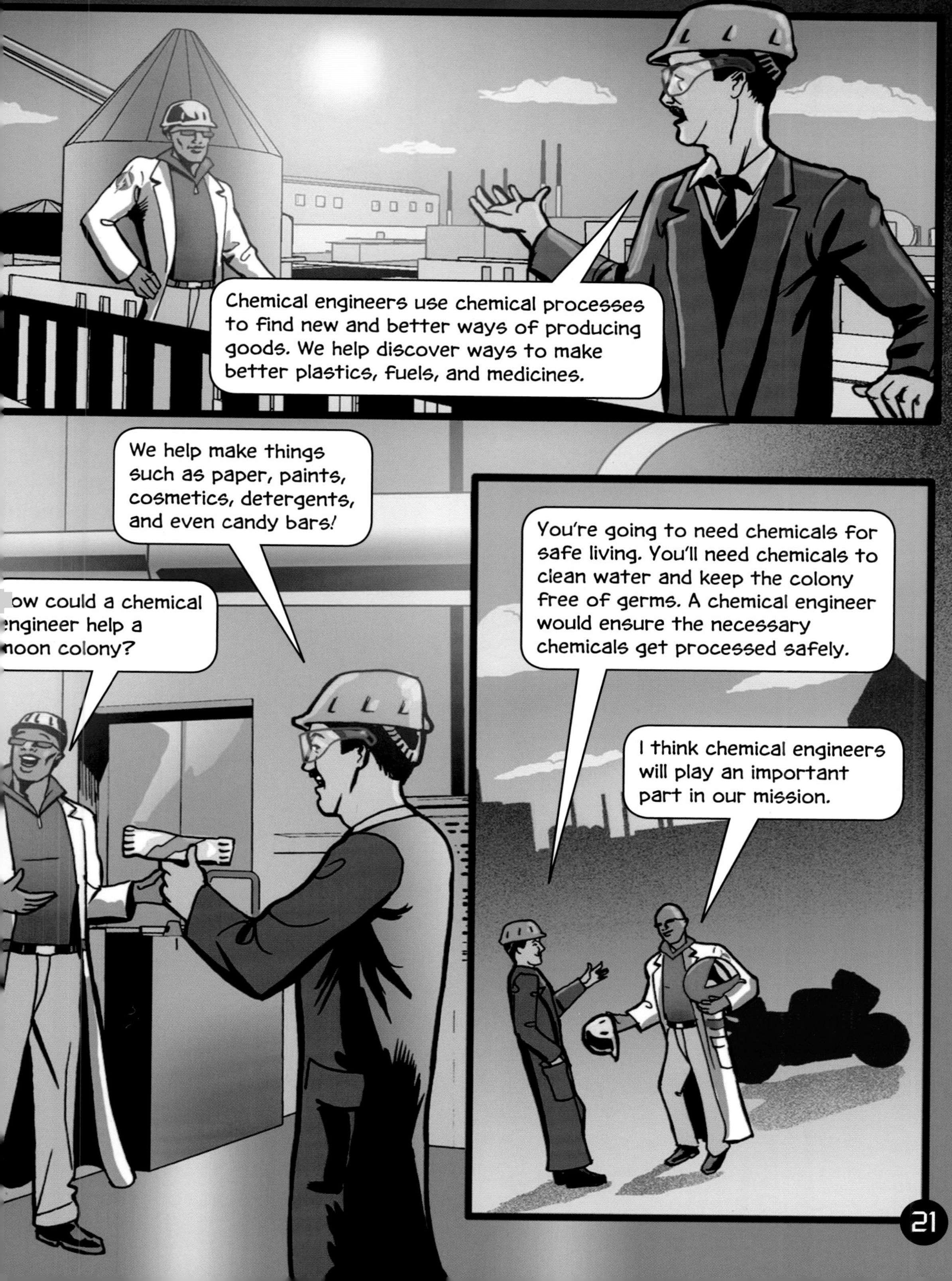

Chemical engineers use chemical processes to find new and better ways of producing goods. We help discover ways to make better plastics, fuels, and medicines.
ow could a chemical ngineer help a oon colony?
We help make things such as paper, paints, cosmetics, detergents, and even candy bars!
You're going to need chemicals for safe living. You'll need chemicals to clean water and keep the colony free of germs. A chemical engineer would ensure the necessary chemicals get processed safely.
I think chemical engineers will play an important part in our mission.

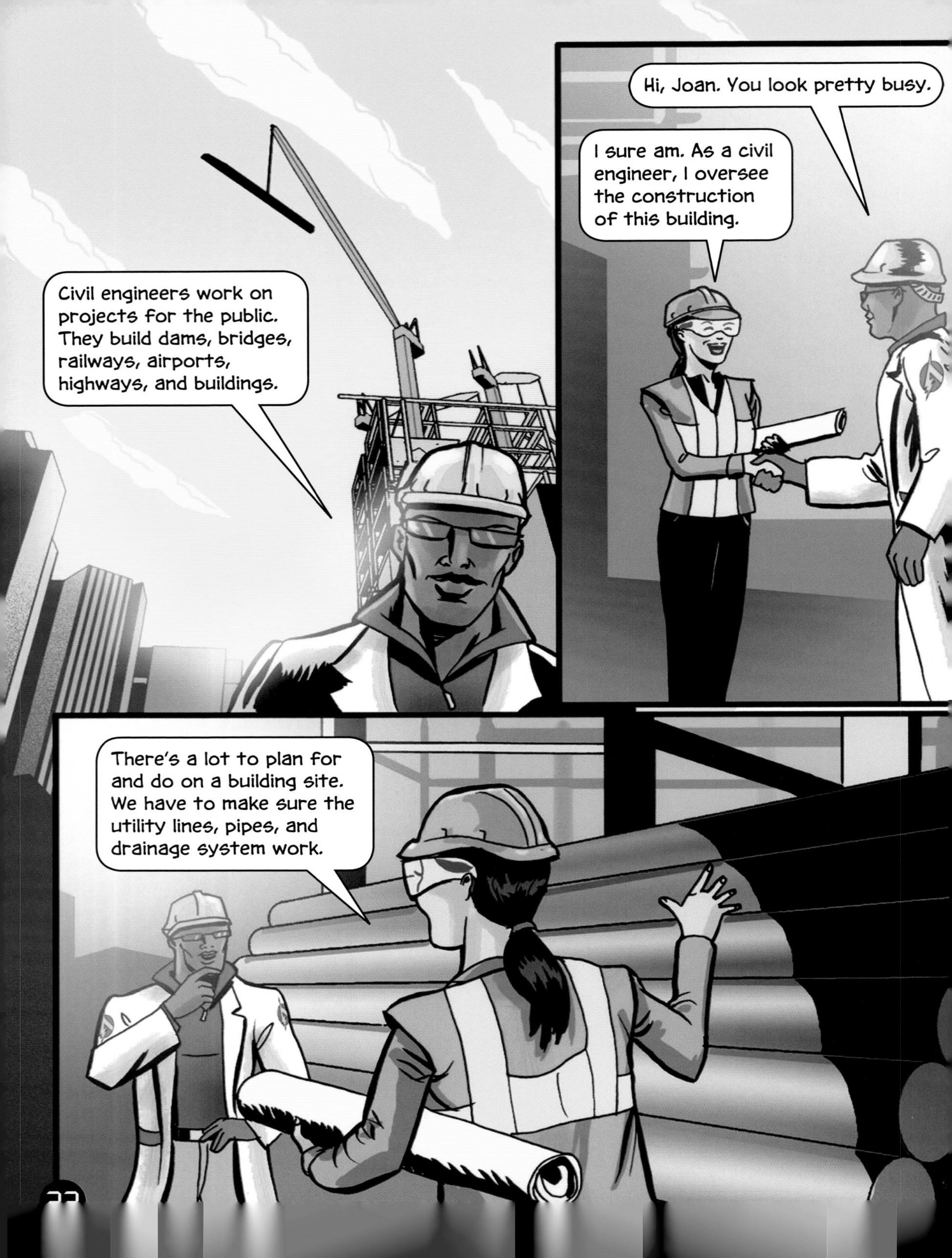
Civil engineers work on projects for the public. They build dams, bridges, railways, airports, highways, and buildings.
Hi, Joan. You look pretty busy.
I sure am. As a civil engineer, I oversee the construction of this building.
There's a lot to plan for and do on a building site. We have to make sure the utility lines, pipes, and drainage system work.

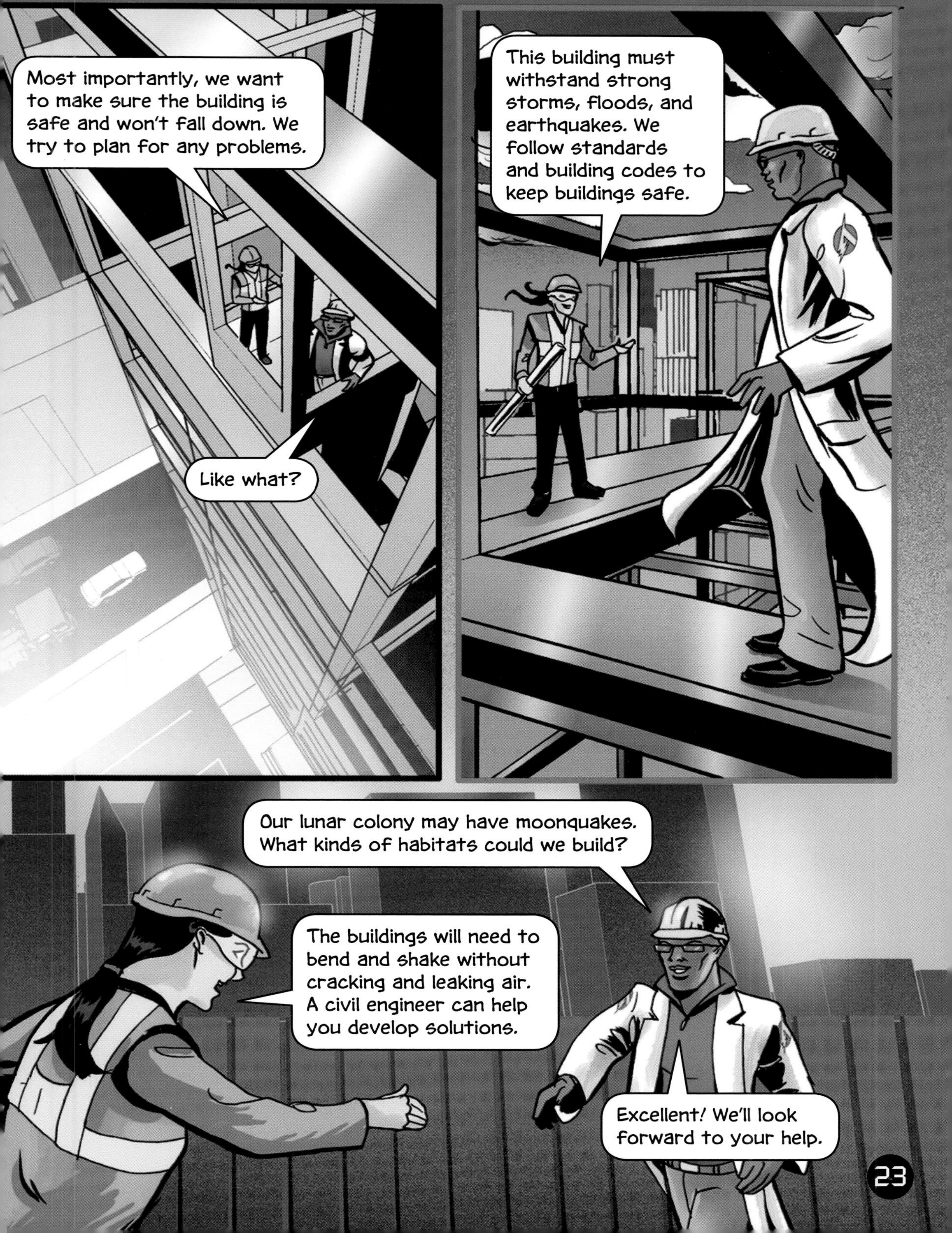
Most importantly, we want to make sure the building is safe and won't fall down. We try to plan for any problems.
Like what?
This building must withstand strong storms, floods, and earthquakes. We follow standards and building codes to keep buildings safe.
Our lunar colony may have moonquakes. What kinds of habitats could we build?
The buildings will need to bend and shake without cracking and leaking air. A civil engineer can help you develop solutions.
Excellent! We'll look forward to your help.

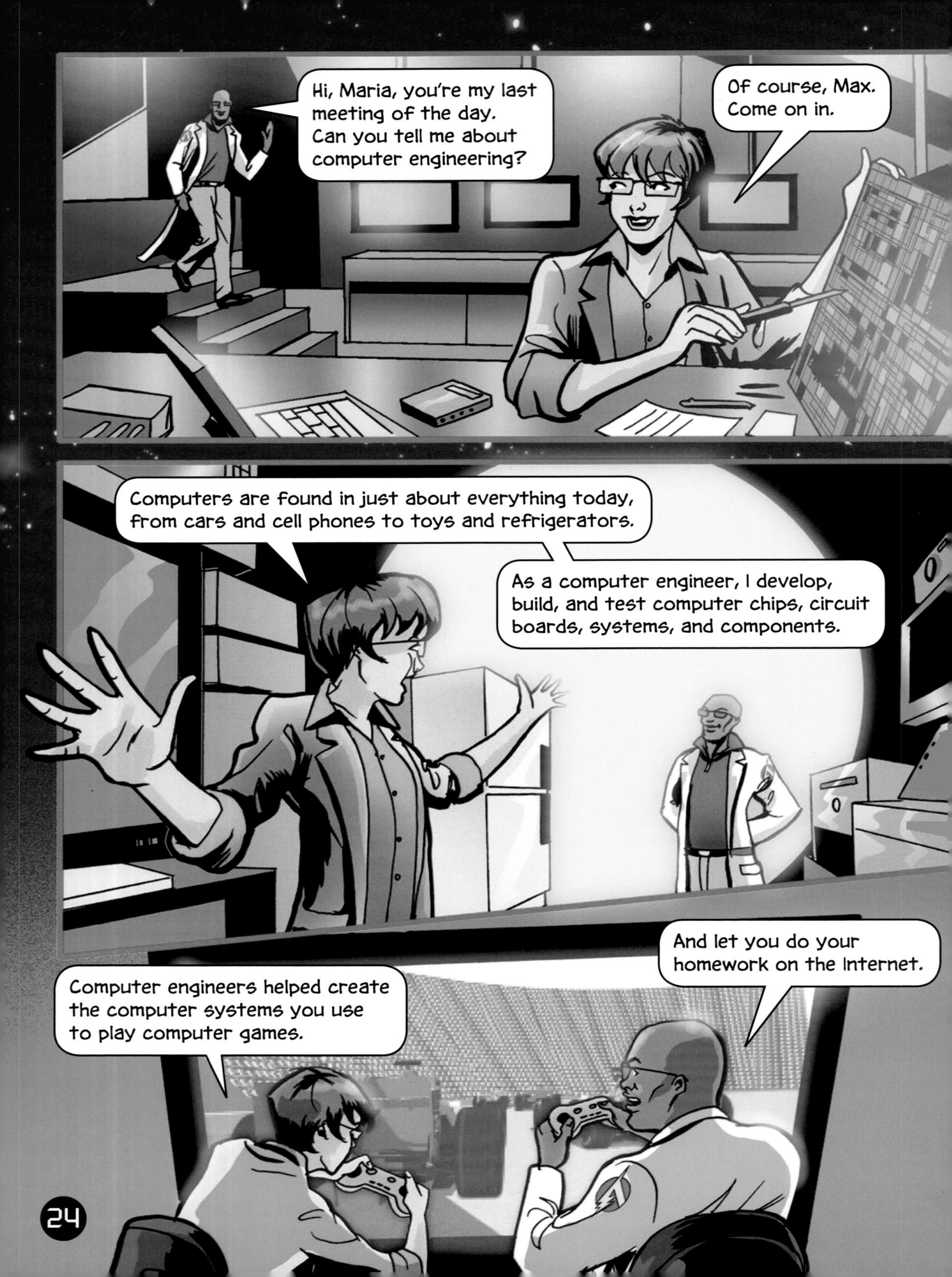
Hi, Maria, you're my last meeting of the day. Can you tell me about computer engineering?
Of course, Max. Come on in.
Computers are found in just about everything today, from cars and cell phones to toys and refrigerators.
As a computer engineer, I develop, build, and test computer chips, circuit boards, systems, and components.
Computer engineers helped create the computer systems you use to play computer games.
And let you do your homework on the Internet.

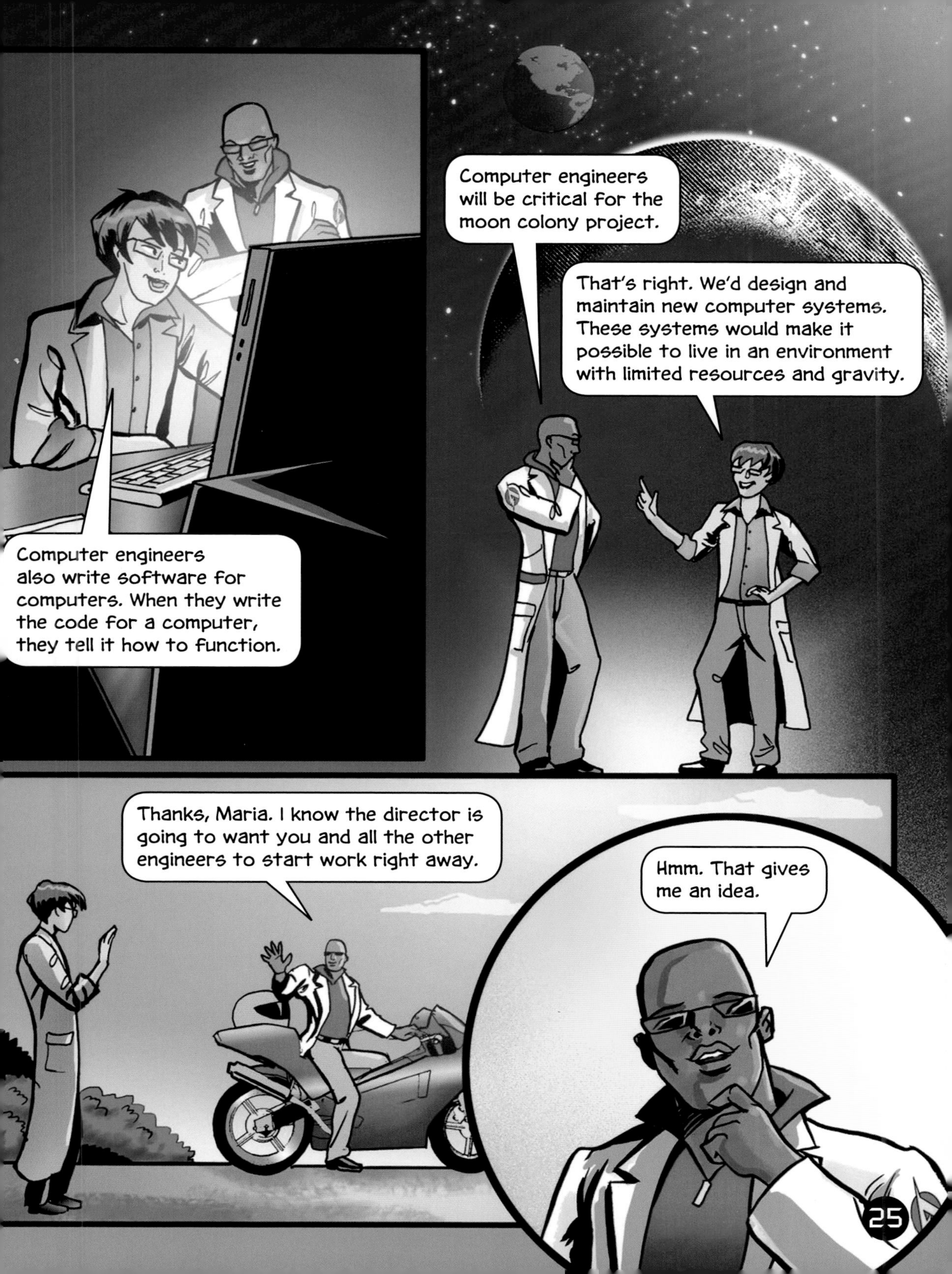
Computer engineers also write software for computers. When they write the code for a computer, they tell it how to function.
Computer engineers will be critical for the moon colony project.
That's right. We'd design and maintain new computer systems. These systems would make it possible to live in an environment with limited resources and gravity.
Thanks, Maria. I know the director is going to want you and all the other engineers to start work right away.
Hmm. That gives me an idea.

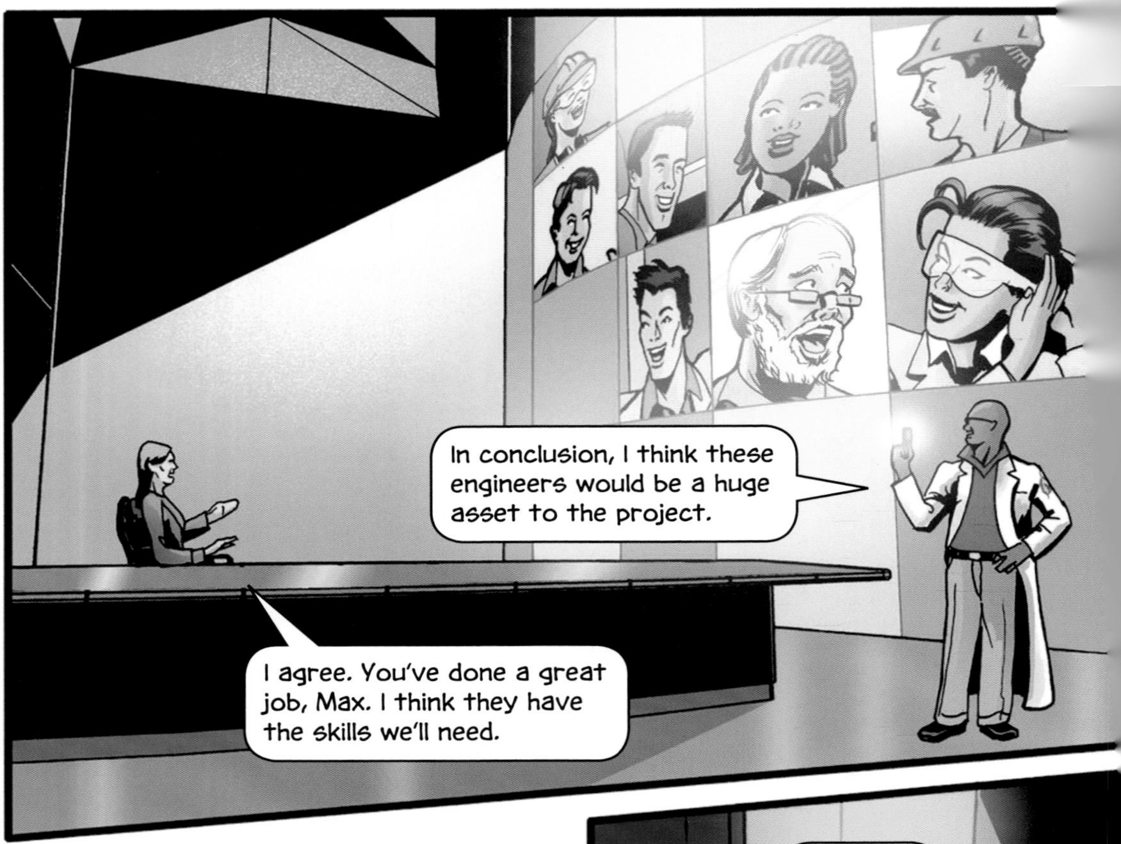
In conclusion, I think these engineers would be a huge asset to the project.
I agree. You've done a great job, Max. I think they have the skills we'll need.

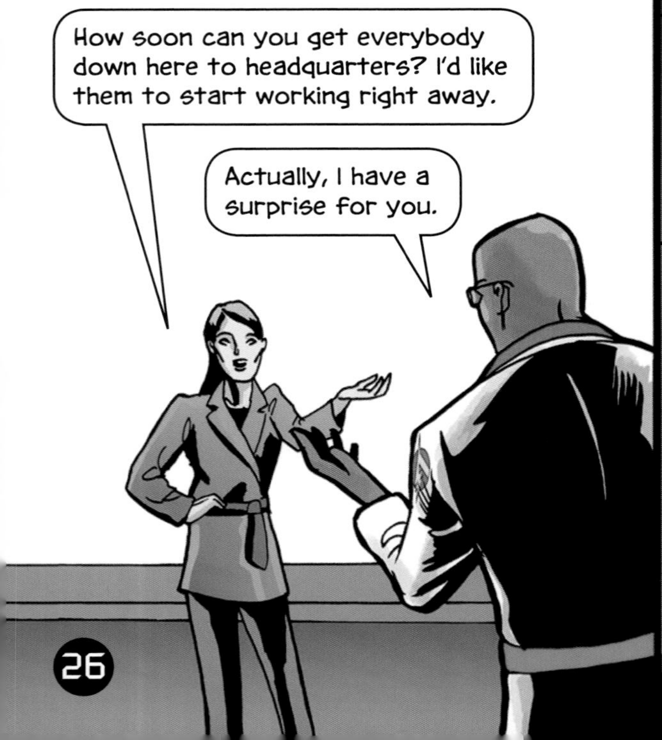
How soon can you get everybody down here to headquarters? I'd like them to start working right away.
Actually, I have a surprise for you.

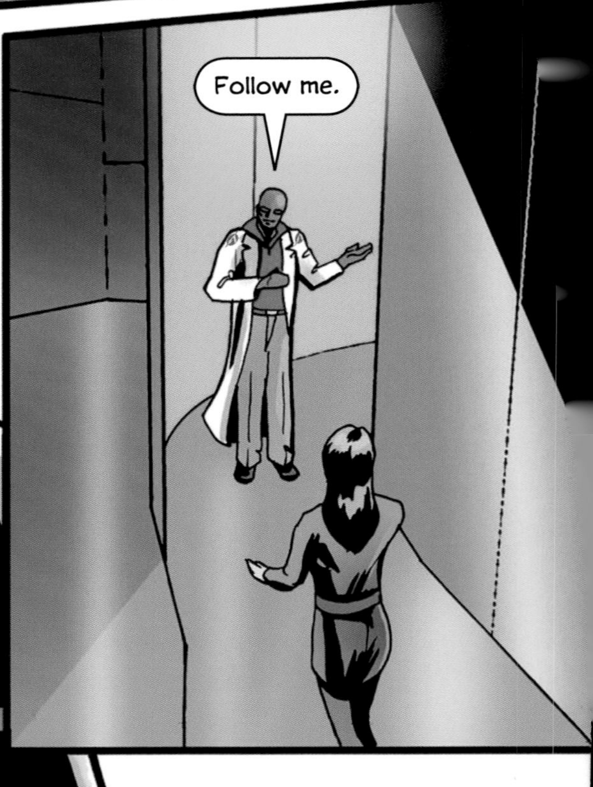
Follow me.

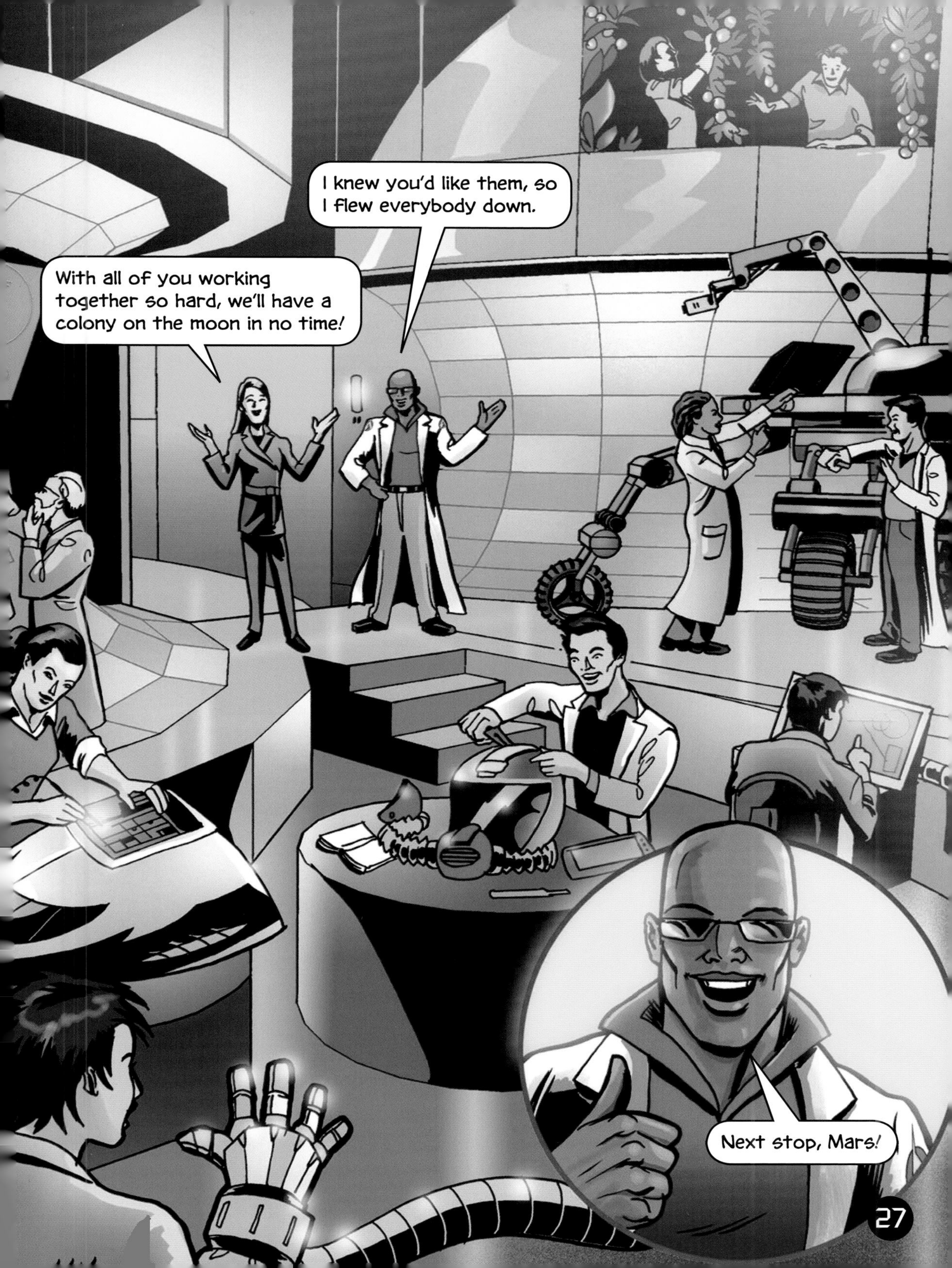
With all of you working together so hard, we'll have a colony on the moon in no time!
I knew you'd like them, so I flew everybody down.
Next stop, Mars!

MORE ABOUT ENGINEERING

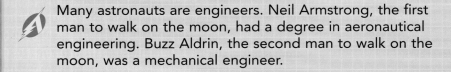

- Many astronauts are engineers. Neil Armstrong, the first man to walk on the moon, had a degree in aeronautical engineering. Buzz Aldrin, the second man to walk on the moon, was a mechanical engineer.

- Materials engineers study how long a metal part can last in a machine or structure. Metal parts can fail due to temperature and stress. A part failure can be deadly if it happens in an airplane engine or a bridge. You can see how stress makes metal fail by bending a paper clip back and forth in the same spot. Eventually it will snap in two.

- Chemical engineers improve medications. They find better ways to produce large amounts of new vaccines. They also figure out how to store medicines longer and how to develop drugs with fewer side effects.

- The pyramids in Egypt are some of the earliest examples of large-scale engineering. The ancient Egyptian Imhotep designed and built the first pyramid for King Djoser more than 4,000 years ago. Imhotep was one of the world's first engineers. He's also the first one we know by name.

- In ancient Rome, civil engineers created large public works. More than 2,000 years ago, Roman engineers built aqueducts. These channels carried clean water into the city. They also built a system of roads to link the cities in their empire.

When people think about engineering wonders, big things come to mind. Civil engineers built the Golden Gate Bridge, the Panama Canal, and the Hoover Dam. They also built the tallest building in the world, Dubai's Burj Khalifa. It stands 2,723 feet (830 meters) tall.

 The National Academy of Engineering listed the greatest engineering achievements of the 20th century that have changed our lives. Use of electricity was number one, followed by the car and the airplane. The Internet was number 13.

MORE ABOUT

SUPER SCIENTIST

Real name: Maxwell J. Axiom
Hometown: Seattle, Washington
Height: 6' 1" Weight: 192 lbs
Eyes: Brown Hair: None

Super capabilities: Super intelligence; able to shrink to the size of an atom; sunglasses give x-ray vision; lab coat allows for travel through time and space.

Origin: Since birth, Max Axiom seemed destined for greatness. His mother, a marine biologist, taught her son about the mysteries of the sea. His father, a nuclear physicist and volunteer park ranger, schooled Max on the wonders of earth and sky.

One day on a wilderness hike, a megacharged lightning bolt struck Max with blinding fury. When he awoke, Max discovered a newfound energy and set out to learn as much about science as possible. He traveled the globe earning degrees in every aspect of the field. Upon his return, he was ready to share his knowledge and new identity with the world. He had become Max Axiom, Super Scientist.

GLOSSARY

aeronautical (ayr-oh-NAW-tuh-kuhl)—having to do with designing and building aircraft

aerospace (AYR-oh-spays)—having to do with designing and building aircraft and spacecraft

artificial (ar-tuh-FI-shuhl)—made by people

astronautical (ass-truh-NAW-ti-kuhl)—having to do with designing and building spacecraft

biology (bye-OL-uh-jee)—the study of plant and animal life

colony (KAH-luh-nee)—a place that is settled by a group of people who live together in the same area

diagnose (dy-ig-NOHS)—to find the cause of a problem

environment (en-VYE-ruhn-muhnt)—the natural world of the land, water, and air

erosion (i-ROH-zhuhn)—the wearing away of land by water or wind

irrigation (ihr-uh-GAY-shuhn)—supplying water to crops using a system of pipes or channels

lunar (LOO-nur)—having to do with a moon

navigation (NAV-uh-gay-shun)—the science of plotting and following a course from one place to another

property (PROP-ur-tee)—quality in a material, such as color, hardness, or shape

technology (tek-NOL-uh-jee)—the use of science to do practical things, such as designing complex machines

vaccine (vak-SEEN)—a medicine that prevents a disease

READ MORE

Enz, Tammy. *Zoom It: Invent New Machines that Move.* Invent It. Mankato, Minn. Capstone Press, 2012.

Graham, Ian. *Massive Monsters and Other Huge Megastructures.* Megastructures. Mankato, Minn.: QEB Pub., 2012.

Gray, Susan Heinrichs. *Bioengineer.* Cool Science Careers. Ann Arbor, Mich.: Cherry Lake Pub., 2011.

Solway, Andrew. *Buildings and Structures.* Science and Technology. Chicago: Raintree, 2011.

INTERNET SITES

FactHound offers a safe, fun way to find Internet sites related to this book. All sites on FactHound have been researched by our staff.

Here's all you do:

Visit *www.facthound.com*

Type in this code: 9781429699372

Check out projects, games and lots more at
www.capstonekids.com

INDEX

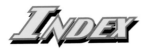